nakaba suzuki presents

CONTENTS

Chapter 329 - Zeldris vs. the Demon Lord

RRRRRUMBLE

So you'd abandon your race...
You'd abandon your own brother?!

Zel. Come with me and bring Gelda with you!
SMACK

Go ahead and leave! I...no longer consider you...my brother...!
Next time we meet will be as enemies!
FWP

Very funny! When that time comes, I won't hesitate to kill you.
I've never once thought of you as my little brother, anyway.
SMIRK

NOW DO YOU REMEMBER? THIS IS THE TRUE NATURE OF THE OLDER BROTHER YOU THINK TO TRUST.
HE'S TRYING TO TRICK YOU.

CHK

SWOOSH
You think your illusions can sway me now?!

BOOM
!!!

NGH...
SSSHHH
SSHHH

If you're turning my past into melodrama, at least make it *good* melodrama.
!
Pfft!
Lie as much as you want, but I know what's really in Meliodas's heart.
ZSH
Even though I'd once convinced myself that he'd betrayed me.

Hey, Zel... Shouldn't you say that to your brother's face?
HEH HEH.
BLUUUSH...
I...I dunno... I'm not... emotionally ready for that yet...
Then how about I tell him for you?
N-No! Don't do that!

YOU DON'T UNDERSTAND HOW IT FEELS FOR A PARENT TO HAVE TO KILL HIS BELOVED SON WITH HIS OWN HANDS.

YOU FOOL!!
DSSSH

Beloved son? Don't make me laugh! I've never once felt loved by you!
If you're going to resort to pity to get your point across, you've really fallen, Father!

HA... HA...HA... DON'T GET COCKY WITH ME!
YOU THINK THE DEMON LORD COULD EVER BE BESTED BY THE LIKES OF YOU?!
ZWAP
As I am now, I may not be as strong as you or Meliodas...
BOOSH

BAM

But this is *the* mind-scape!
REEL
ZSSH
Here I have a fighting chance!
Just as Meliodas has someone he'd risk his life for...
...I also...
...have someone I could never give up on!

CLANG
YOU THINK THE DEMON LORD HIMSELF WOULD YIELD TO A WEAKLING WHO'S UNDER THE THUMB OF SOME WOMAN?!
CLANG
CLANG
CLANG
CLANG
CLANG
CLANG
CLANG
CLANG
DSH
CRIK
!!!

You could never under-stand...
...how the joy of loving someone and being loved...
...can bring forth tremendous strength.
Y-You'd better not tell Meliodas I said that!
BAH
Yeah, yeah.

Father. Right now, your pride is crumbling and your heart is weakened.
And the reason why is clear.
You've suffered a crushing defeat against Meliodas before...
...and even though you're the Demon Lord, you're losing to him *again*!

YOU DARE SUGGEST THE DEMON LORD WOULD LOSE TWICE?!
CLEARLY YOU'RE NOT SEEING WHAT'S GOING ON OUTSIDE!

ZASH

TAK
I know...

ZSSSH

BECAUSE
I TRUST
MY BIG
BROTHER!

YOU TOO WOULD DEFY YOUR OWN FATHER?!
AARGH...
I told you...
...I'd beat you!

"OMINOUS NEBULA"!!!!

DSH
RRRUMBLE
ゴロゴロ

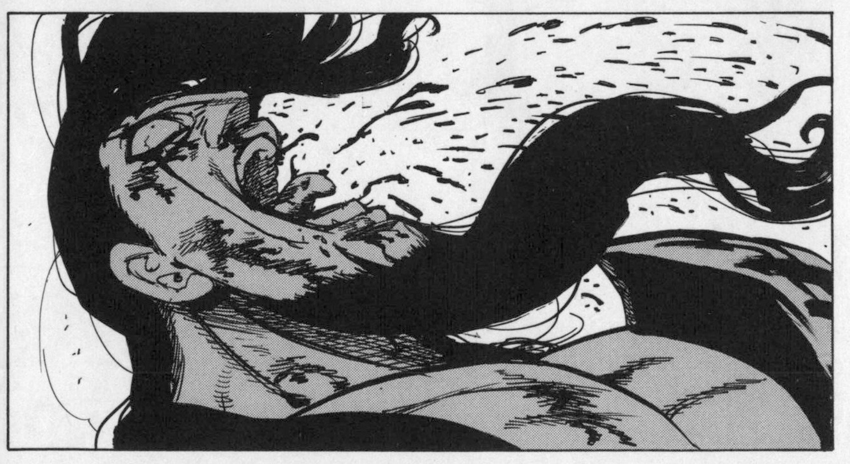

SPLAT

BLORP

SWAY
GLOP

BLINK
Ah!

Zel!!
Gelda! You're back!

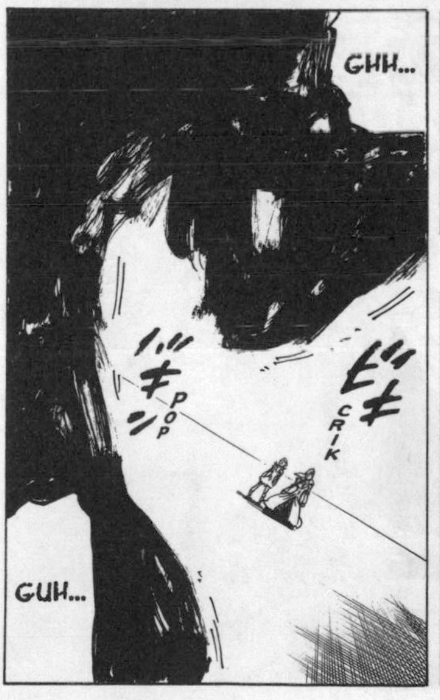
GHH...
CRIK
POP
GUH...

GWAAAAAAAH!!!!
POP
SNAP

Chapter 330 - The Struggle

What happened to him? He looks like he's in pain!

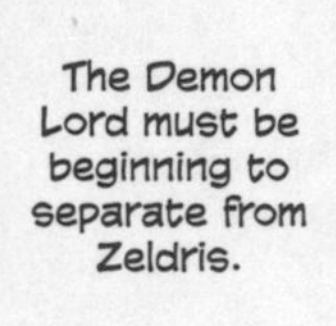
The Demon Lord must be beginning to separate from Zeldris.

CRUNCH
SNAP
GUH... AAA-AH!

BWOOSH

ZEL!!

!!
MY VESSEL! I WON'T LET IT GO!
GLORP

Ah!

?!
SHH

Heh Heh! ♬ Too bad for you. ♬

...!!!
Here you go. ♬
NICE SAVE, BAN!

Thanks!
You owe me ten rounds of Aberdeen Ale! ♬
BUMP

Thank good-ness!
Thank you... really!
TWITCH

Uuh... I...

...!
ZSH

You did it, Zeldris!
You beat Father!

BOOMF
Hmph. Of course I did.
JIGGLE

HEH.
Well, now. You sure are a boobs kinda guy.
YOU BURROWED YOUR FACE IN HER CHEST WHILE IN THE MINDSCAPE, TOO.
N-N... No, I'm not!

HOW DARE YOUUU!
DSSH
VSH
Aaah! He's running away!
Ha.
WIT-NESS...
...ME!

BOOM
HE EXPLODED AND SCATTERED HIMSELF!
What's he doing ...?
Oh, no...!
BLOP
BLOP
BLOP
BLOP
BLOP
BLOP
SPLAT
ZSSHH

BLOP
BLOP
BLOP

ZSH
ZSH
BLOP
BLOP

CRACK
CRACK
CRACK
CRACK

The fallen Commandments are taking over every living thing they touch.
And that's not all! Even the rocks and hills!

RRRUMBLE
Merlin... What is he after?
There's no mis-taking it.

Now that Meliodas and Zeldris have rejected him...
...he's planning on making the very ground of Britannia his new vessel.
DSH

DOOO
DORRR
RMMM

CRUMBLE
CRUMBLE
ZSH
ZSH
ZSH
ZSH
CRUMBLE

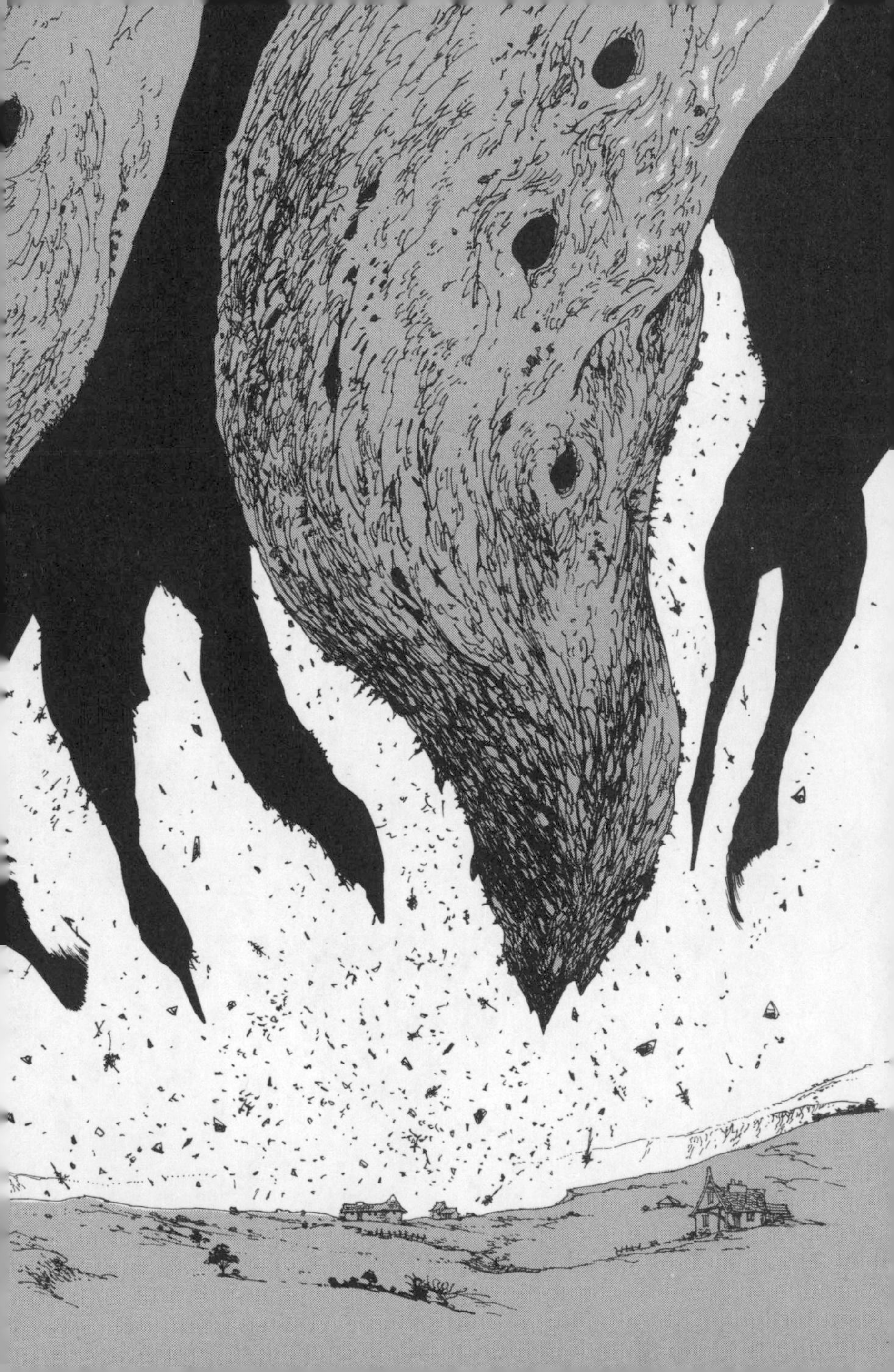

DSSH
BSSH

FWOOSH

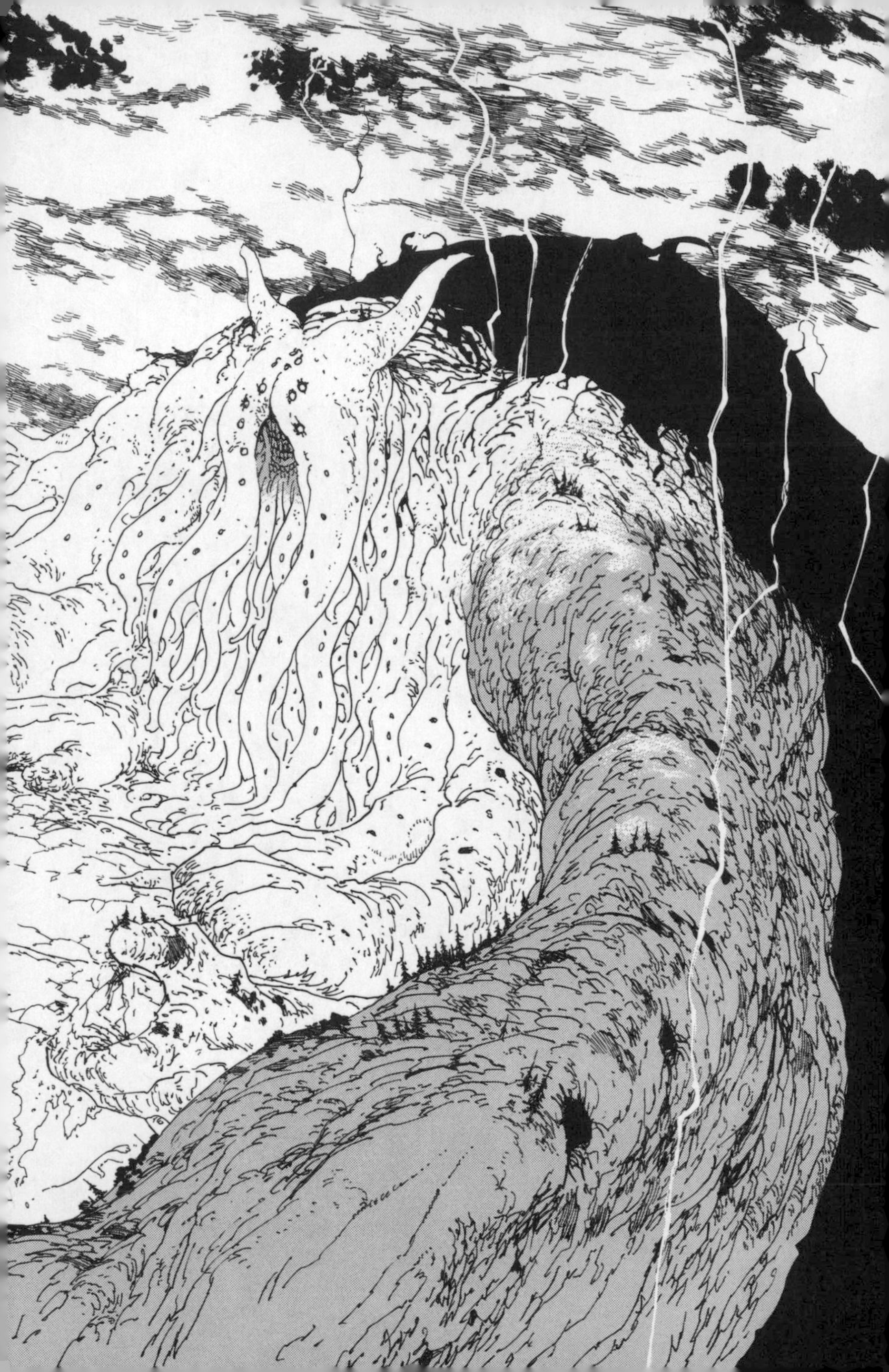

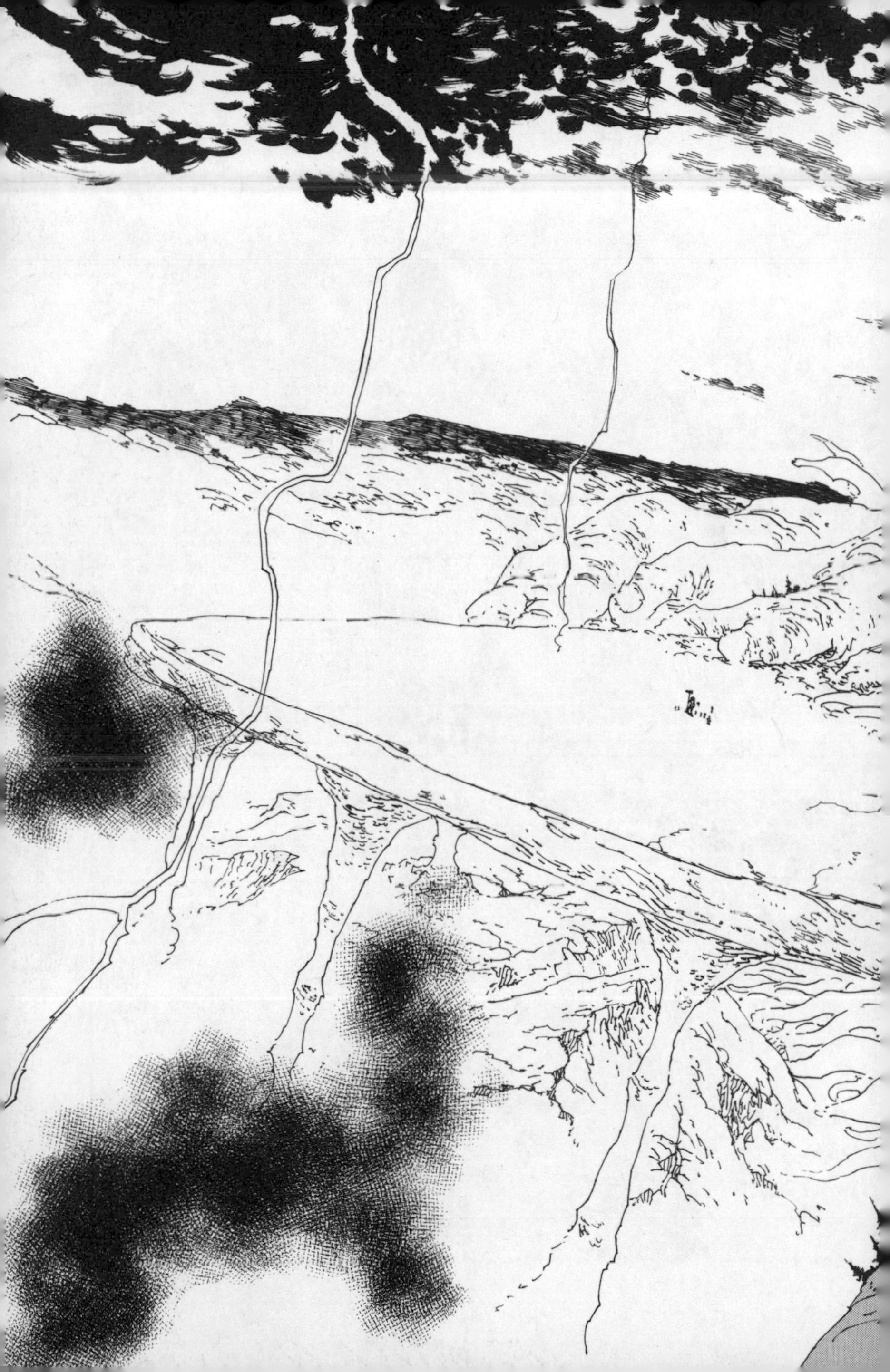

CRACK
SNAP
Don't dilly-dally, Mom!
Everyone'll be dead before the great hero Hawk-sama gets there!
BOAR HAT
CLIP
CLOP
SNAP CRACK

SNOINK!
Huh?
Look ahead?

WAAAH! WH-WHAT THE?!
WHAT THE HECK IS *THAT*?!
SNOINK!

ON SECOND THOUGHT, TURN BACK! I CAN'T DO IT! NO WAY! NO WAY!
RRRUMBLE
DANGER! DANGER! DANGER!!
CLOP
CLIP

What a frightening sight!

Please get away from there, Meliodas!

Shoot. How are we supposed to fight a monster like that?!
Gil...
I'll stay with you to the end... Veronica-sama!

It's all... over.

Elaine-sama, are we gonna die?
...!!

I SEE THE FACES OF BRITANNIA'S RESIDENTS CRUMPLED IN FEAR.
ALL BECAUSE OF THE SINFUL FOLLIES YOU HAVE COMMITTED.

TREMBLE IN FEAR! RESIGN TO YOUR DEATHS!
WOOOO
CRACK
THERE IS NO GREATER CRIME THAN DEFYING THE DEMON LORD!!

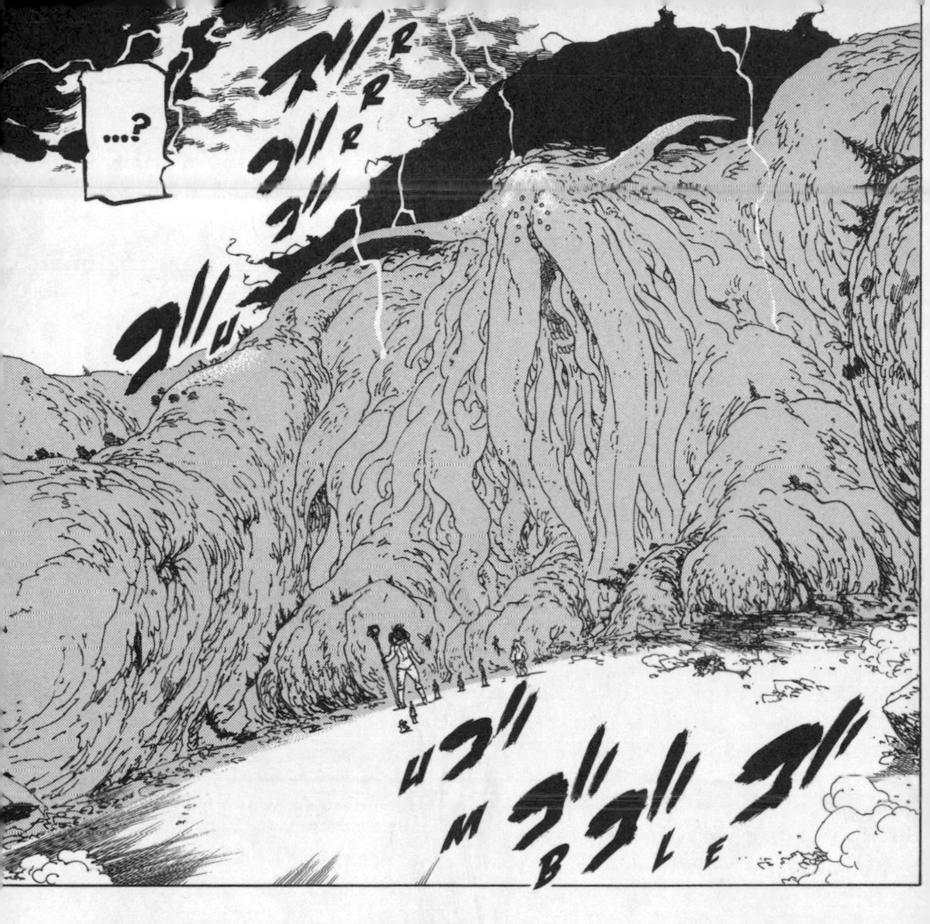
...?
RRR
RUMBLE
RUMBLE

WHY DO YOU ALL LOOK LIKE THAT?
TELL ME. WHY?!
In this fight...
...you don't stand a chance, Father.

RUMBLE
RUMBLE

I DESPISE OLD MEN WHO CANNOT TAKE A HINT.
'KAY? ☆

Sorry.
I have a wedding to plan after all of this.

I'm not afraid...
...because all my friends are here!

RRRUMBLE

Your body is quite broken down.
Was that spur of the moment substitute the best you could come up with?
THAT WAS THE ULTIMATE IDIOCY, DEMON LORD!
So, yeah.
Let's take this guy down. ♫

EVERY-
ONE...
LET'S
GO!!

Chapter 331 - Mortal Enemies

ZSH

"DEATH ZERO."

NGH!
I WILL CRUSH YOU FROM EXISTENCE AND SCATTER YOUR REMAINS.
ZSH
ZSH
ZSH
HOW DARE PUNY BUGS SUCH AS YOURSELVES HOPE TO DEFY A MOUNTAIN?
ZSH

I crush down... mountains... before... lunch!
Ha!

Hmph !!
Take that !
BOOM
CRACK
HA... FUTILE. A GOD CANNOT FEEL PAIN OR FEAR.

... Hngh!
ZSH
ZSH

SO YOU CAN'T FEEL PAIN OR FEAR, HUH?
THAT MEANS YOU'RE DEAD. ♫

THOOM
...!

YOU ARE MERE PAWNS OF THE HOLY WAR!
YOU SHOULD HAVE ACTED AS SUCH AND FOUGHT AT THE BIDDING OF THE GODS.
バチ ZAP
バチバチ ZAP ZAP

I... hate fight-ing...
But...if it means defeating you... I'll gladly fight...!
YOU ACTUALLY MEAN TO ATTACK A GOD?
WAKE UP FROM YOUR DELUSION!
THOOM
I'll do whatever I can...to protect what I must.
Be-cause I'm...a greedy king!

MERLIN!

Get ready. I'll be sure to let you sleep it off for a week after this.
SWF

DASH
"POWER LIMIT BREAK"

!!
N... No way. Magic's coursing through my body!
DAUGHTER OF BÉRIALIN! YOU'RE NOT SATISFIED SIMPLY DECEIVING THE GODS, AND NOW MEAN TO...
BAM
A God has no right to comment on the path I have chosen!!

"Trillion Dark."
"Final Prominence."
"Kill Switch."
"Jet Hammer."
"Spear of Judgment."
"Crazy Rush."

WOOOO
IDIOTS.
IN THE FACE OF MY "RULER" MAGIC...
You're the idiot. With Gowther's "Kill Switch" ...
...we can turn your magic off.

SNAP

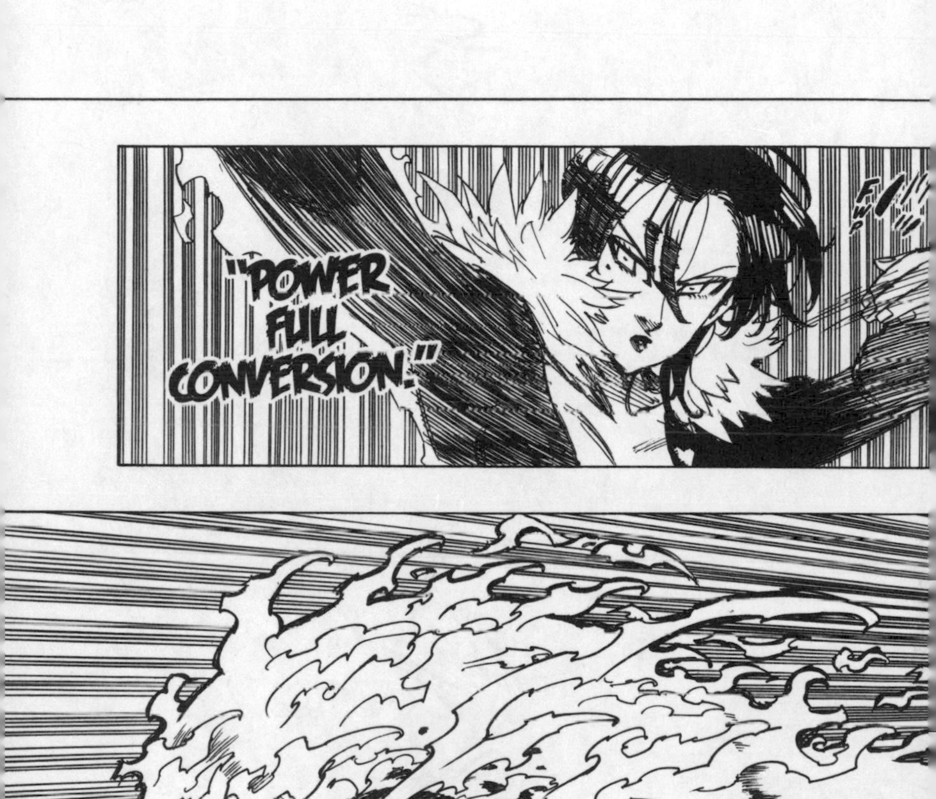
FWP!!
"POWER FULL CONVERSION."

B...BE GONE!!
GLOP

ZSSH

IT IS NO USE.
NO MATTER HOW MUCH YOU STRUGGLE, YOU CANNOT ERASE THE FEELINGS ETCHED IN OUR HEARTS!!

BOOM

MY SONS!!
YOU WOULD ABANDON ME?!
TIIIING

"FULL COUNTER"
OOH... SON...
YOUR STU-PIDITY SAVED ME!
ZLOOSH
!!!
AN ILLU-SION ...
SSHHH

!
I'm glad you're such an irredeemable dirtbag.
Now I can beat you to a pulp without hesitation!
WOOOOO

"FULL COUNTER"
TING
MELIO-DAS?!
WHOOSH

With every strike of "Full Counter," its power and size just gets greater and greater.

RRRRRRRUMMB
BBLL
...THERE'S NO TELLING WHAT WILL HAPPEN TO BRITANNIA!
FLAP
FLAP
Is this angle good, Merlin?
Melio-das... Do it!

TING
CRMBL
"FULL COUNTER"
So long, Father!!

THE SEVEN DEADLY SINS' COMBO MOVE.

"NEMESIS"

YOU WILL COME TO REGRET THIS, MELIODAS.
THE AGE OF LIGHT AND DARK WILL END, AND WHAT YOU HAVE INVITED IS...
...WELL, YOU AL-READY KNOW.

It's just as I'd wanted.

Chapter 332 - The Price

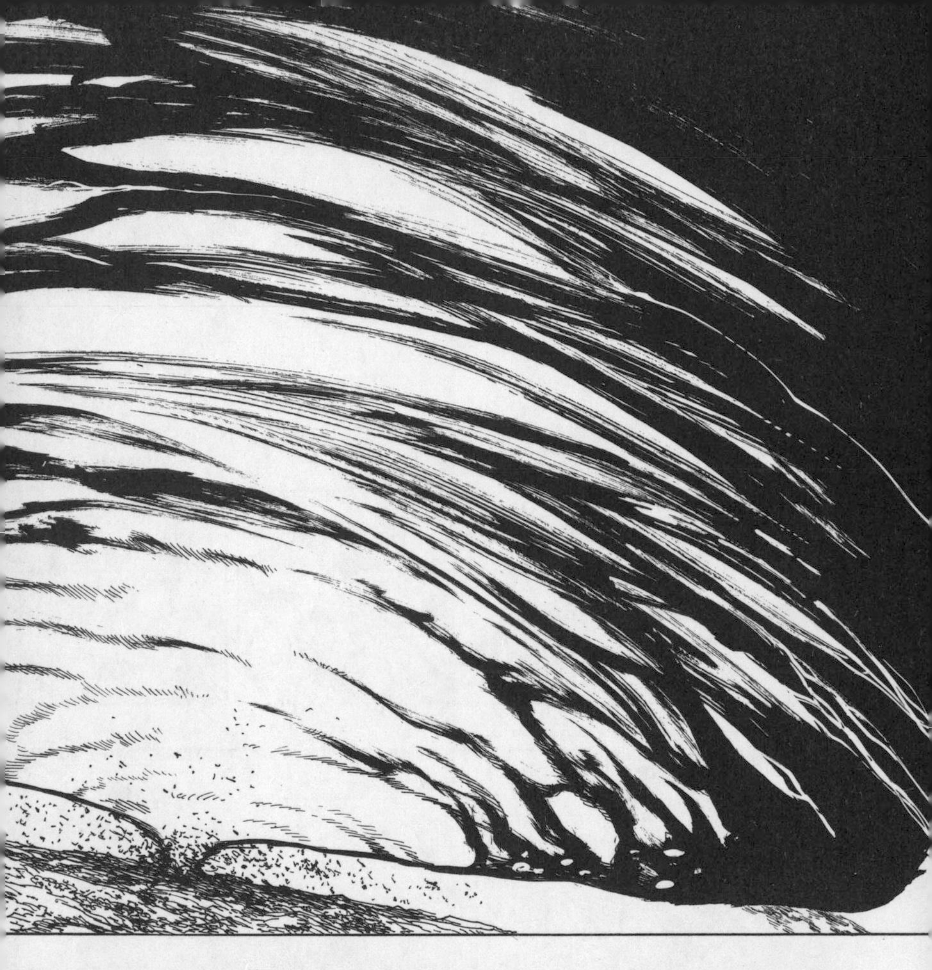

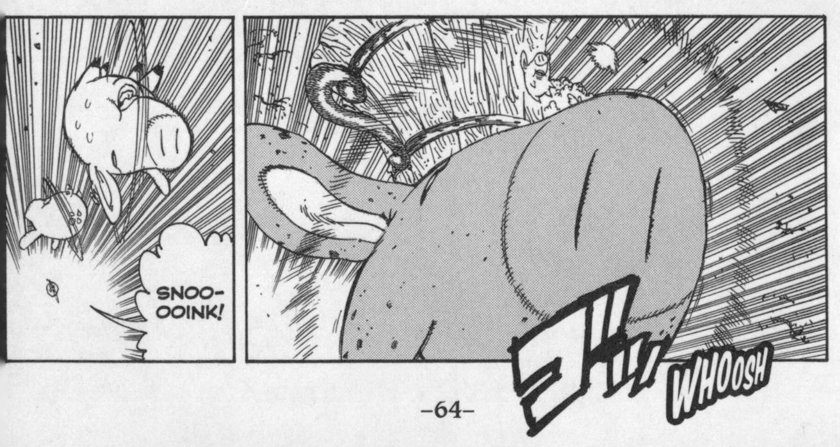
WHOOSH
SNOO-
OOINK!

BOOOSH

DSH
DSH
DSH
DSH
DSH
DSH

KRAK
CRUMBLE

Zel! Zel?!
Answer me!
Gelda, look up!
!
I'm glad I made it!
I don't need your help!
KRK
KRK
PLOP
PLOP
PLOP
PLOP
PLOP

Every-
one,
hold
on!

KSSHT

SSHHH

Thanks, Eliza-beth.
HEH HEH!

Alley...oof! It's no use. I have no strength left.
THAT IS THE NATURAL RESULT OF HAVING UNLEASHED POWER BEYOND OUR LIMITS THANKS TO MERLIN'S MAGIC.
I really do feel like I could sleep for a week...

How about you, Gowther?
I AM A DOLL. I FEEL NO PAIN AND I CAN STILL MOVE.
CLICK
CLICK
CLICK
CREAK
CREAK
BUT I MAY FALL APART IF I PUSH MYSELF.
CRUNCH

Hey... Ban.
Yeah?

How do you get married?
Idiot. ♫

I'm not an idiot. I'm basically your brother-in-law now.
This sucks. ♫
Both of you, quit squabbling!

Meliodas. Tell me how you did it.
Everything okay, Zel?
FLAP

The combo move you guys released was powerful enough to have wiped out Britannia...
TMP
How were you able to make it so only the Demon Lord took the force of it?

There's your answer.
ZSH

?!!

Is that...a blob of water?
It's the magic lake that stores limitless magic. We were able to pull it off because this thing absorbed all the excess power.
What a strange sight. A lake that can continue to persist even after losing the basin that contained it...

I'm impressed you were able to make that call so quickly.

That was thanks to Merlin's advice. Right, Merlin?
That woman's too crafty.

Captain! Fire at the Demon Lord, aiming for the lake!

C-CAP-TAIN!

Th... This can only mean...
How is this possible?

But I thought we'd defeated the Demon Lord?!
The Commandments haven't gone away!

Conceit of the highest order.
GRRK
HAAH... HAAH...
SWAY
SWAY
Tch. What the heck is this?

RIGHT?
Centuries fly by in no time!
YEAH.
I wouldn't say they *fly by*...
Oh no!
We were dealing with a God, after all. Even if we managed to defeat him, he's too tough to completely annihilate.
Even after decades or even centuries, his power could still revive.
Right, Meliodas?
Don't worry. There's a way to destroy him.

It can't be!
Is that... really possible?

Yeah.

Stand back, Zel.
What are you going to do?

SHIVER

HAAH!
ZSSSSH

That form... That magic!
I don't believe it!
It's on par with Father's... No, it's well beyond it!
Don't tell me this is a manifestation of your own power!
WHOOSH
FWAAAH
ZWP

SWF
RRRRUMBLE
ゴゴゴ…
I'll throw all my power at them to wipe out the Demon Lord!

RUMBLE
ガラ ガラ
RUMBLE

RUMBLE
RUMBLE
RUMBLE
RUMBLE
RUMBLE
RRRMBL
THE TWO DEMON LORDS' POWERS ARE RESONATING STRONGLY. AND THIS IS THE SIDE EFFECT OF THAT!
WHAAH!
CRACK
Eek!
GRAB
Be gone!

W-Wait! Are you sure about this?
With this much power, you could take our father's place!
Yeah, I could.
...!
I could rule the Demon World with fear just like Father did.

But that isn't my wish. Is it yours?
I doubt it is. Your wish is to build a peaceful world where you can live with Gelda, isn't it?

You're right.
SLIP
Power isn't what we want.

ZAP
ZAP
THE AGE OF LIGHT AND DARK WILL END, AND WHAT YOU HAVE INVITED IS...
...WELL, YOU ALREADY KNOW.

You're right. No matter what age comes next...
Those who fight with us and follow our ideals will continue to resist.

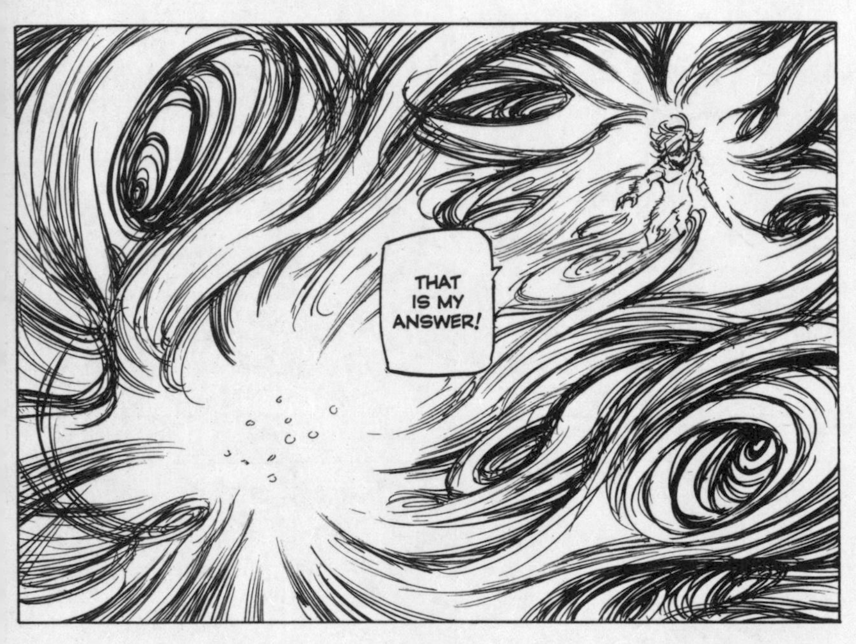
THAT IS MY ANSWER!

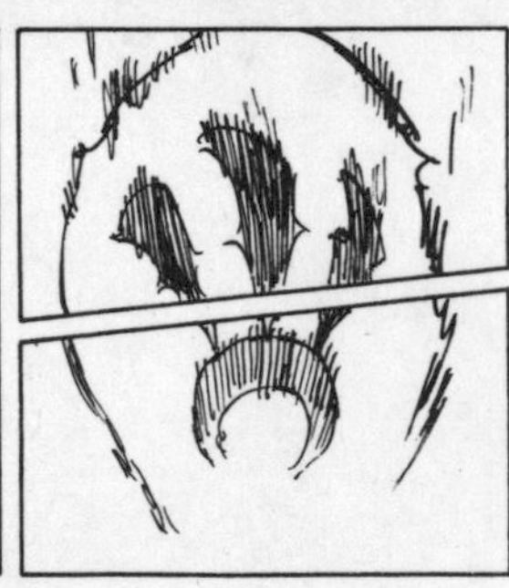

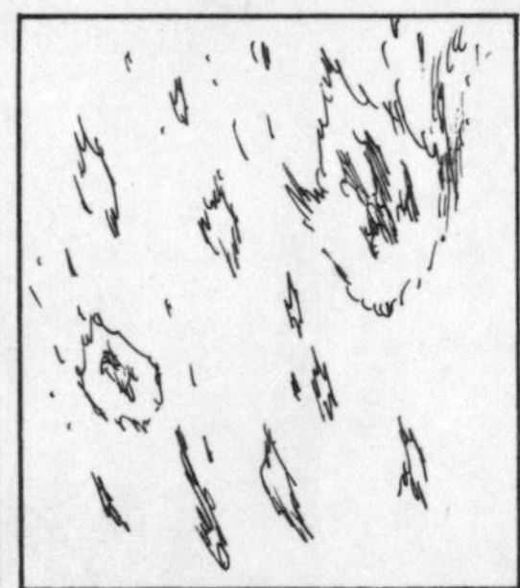

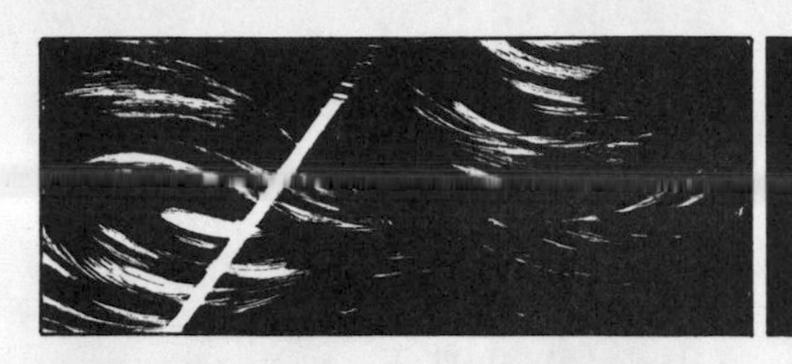

It's all over.
Yeah.

Well, well, well! Today calls for a celebratory drink!
HEH HEH
How about it, Zel? Will you join us?

Hmph. I don't want to be around people...

Yeah? Well, I won't force you, then.

...But if it's just the two of us, I'll think about it...
Huh?

Granted, you have to pick up the tab.

Chapter 333 - Arrogance, Overeating, and Scars

There they go.

Well... You guys had better go, too.
Every-one's waiting.

DRIP
...!

You can't just stand there forever.
Come back... with us.

Don't say... just us.
You're coming, too.

I'm sorry... I can't move my body anymore.
FWOOSH
CRUMBLE
FRSH
CRUMBLE
FSH
FSH
FSH
It looks like this... is the end of the road for me.

But...I have no regrets for the life I led.
FWSH
FWSH
CRMBL
Everyone... Thank you for coming into my life.

Gowther-kun...
I always enjoyed our talks.

...!
King-kun... Diane-san.
I'm sorry I won't be able to attend your wedding, but...I wish you all the happiness in the world.

Eliza-beth-sama.
Give my best to His Highness, Hendy-kun, and the others.
Mael-san.
Thank you for taking care of us to the very end.

Ban-san.
Try not to drink too much.
Cap-tain.
I owe my life to you. You're my very best friend.
ZSH
ZSH

Merlin-
san.

I've always loved you.
And I know it's not only because you remind me so much of Rosa.
You never treated me any different than anyone else.

Hmph.

You give me too much credit.
How do you know I didn't only see you as an interesting specimen to study?

Even if that's all it was, I'm still happy.
FWOOSH

As long as it meant I got to take up even a little corner of your heart...

...Too late...
GRIP

It's too late for anything now.
We can't turn back time.

...?

Escanor. I wish you'd found me sooner.
3,000 years sooner, even.

Merlin ?

No matter what, I'm on your side.
No matter what you decide to do... or what kind of crimes you commit...

...!

You mean you know...?!

No... It's just a hunch.
CRACKLE
CRACKLE
After all, since the day we met, you've always had the saddest eyes.

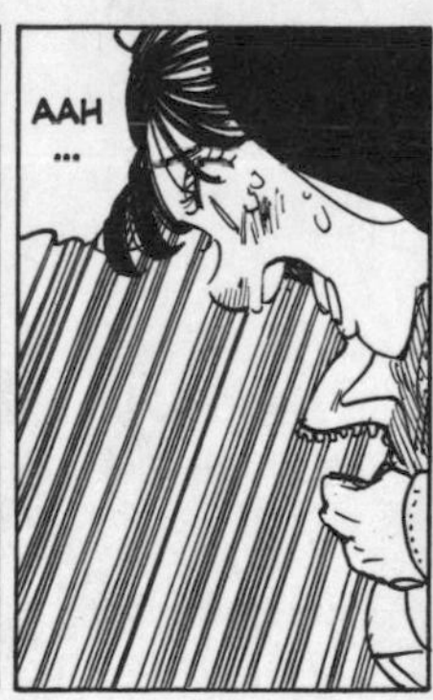
AAH ...

ES-CANOR... YOUR BODY!!
Oh.

It looks like my time is up.
CRUMBLE
CRUMBLE

FWOOSH
Take care, everyone.
This could be dangerous... so please keep your distance.

I'll see you off, Escanor.

I don't... want to...say good-bye...

SMILE

Goodbye, Merlin-sa—

CLACK

?!
CLACK
CLACK
It's too danger-ous! Stay back...!

SSHH

SIZZLE
WOOO
CRACKLE
CRACKLE
SIZZLE
SIZZLE

I wasn't able to return your feelings, but...

...the least I could do was burn into my flesh...
...proof that you existed. Proof of the only man to ever love me.

CRMBL
ボロ

"Yours is a lonely love; the finest wine to inebriate the heart."
"But I cannot be the chalice that will hold you."
"O, Lord..."
ボロ
SNAP

"I pray that another chalice appear that can embrace that love."

SSSHHH

Sleep well, Escanor.

Bonus Story: From One Perspective

Continued on page 124

Chapter 334 - The End of an Era

That huge, ominous magic is gone! It's like it was never even here!
This must mean...

The sun...
The disaster's over!
Are we... saved?

Yeah.
They did it.

Lord Hen-drick-son! Jericho!
Oh! Guila! And Drey-fus-sama!

Let's get back to Liones!

KING BARTRA!!

HAAAH!
HAAAH!
W...
What is it?!

The Seven Deadly Sins have defeated the Demon Lord and returned home!
Eliza-beth-sama is safe and with them as well!

Y...You don't say.
That's won-derful!

WAAH!
We shall mark today a new holiday in Britannia and hold a festival!
Let us welcome The Seven Deadly Sins home at once!
W
OOOOOOOO!

Wait, Gil! Where on earth are you going?!
Your favorite hero is coming home! At least be there to say—

!!

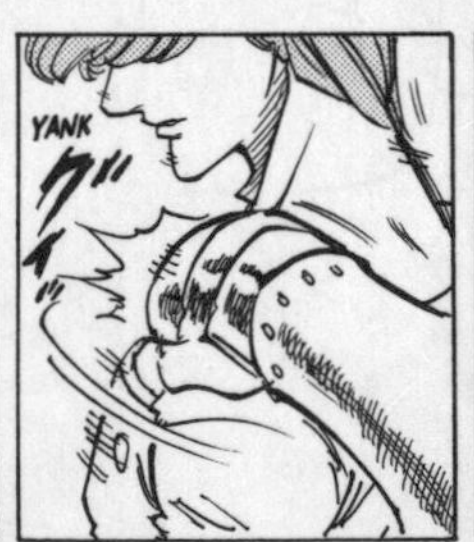
YANK

CLANG
I said wait!!
CLANG

It's a real shame... about Lord Escanor...

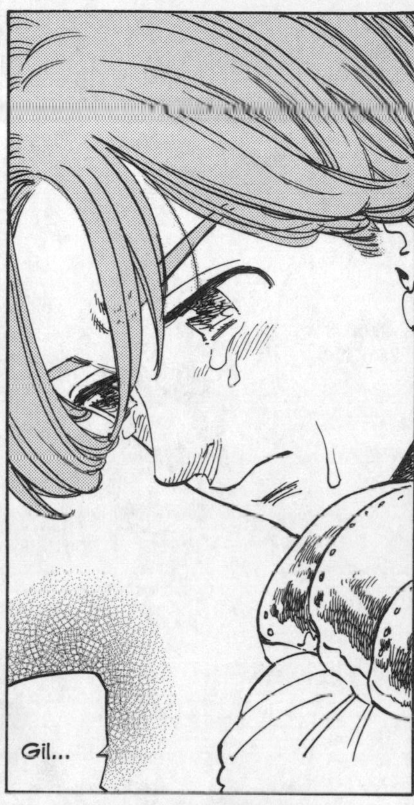
Gil...

When I think of how Meliodas and the others must be feeling...
...I can't begin to imagine what to say when I see them.

Yeah... I hear ya.
...Lis-ten.

Why don't we spend tonight drinking, just the three of us?
Yeah? I'll tell His Highness, then.
Thanks for being there for me, guys...

I can't believe the legendary Seven Deadly Sins lost one of their members.
Yeah. That'd be like if our gang lost you, Howzer.
What?! Why me?!
It was just an example. Don't take it personally.

Lord Escanor was ready to die. He was smiling when said he would gladly stake his life for his friends.

That's not some-thing just anyone can do.

Man, I look up to the guy.
I wanna become a Holy Knight like that, too, someday.
That's so conceited.
RAWR
WHAT'S WRONG WITH LOOKING UP TO SOMEBODY?!

Heh. You're right.
He even said so himself... That there's a shining future ahead of us.

GLANCE
B-By the way... Are we really drinking at my house?
It was *your* idea to go drink, so it only makes sense.
Yeah, but... I wish we could drink at *your* house sometime, Howzer.
No way! My mom and pop would get all excited and up in our business.

Is there something inconvenient about us coming over?
SHWP
Oh, I know, I know! Griamore actually has a secret child he's hiding from us!

...
SIGH

CLINK
To The Seven Deadly Sins!
And to the tomorrow that they protected!
To The Lion Sin of Pride!

Aww, I'm sorry to have to tell you.

ZSH
Apparently, an imbalance between light and dark brings...
...times of chaos.

CLATTER

V...
BADUM
Vivian?!

You...! You still won't quit it with Gil?!
F-Forget that! I thought you were killed by Ludoshel!

Ah, yes. Back in those heavenly ruins.
It's true I was run through by a Goddess's sword.

TA-DAH
FWP FWP FWP FWP FWP FWP
But!!
Like the immortal Phoenix, I came back to life!
Through the power of love. ♡

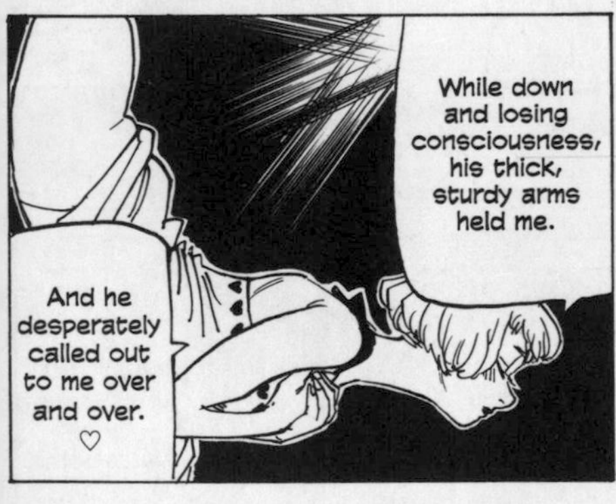
While down and losing consciousness, his thick, sturdy arms held me.
And he desperately called out to me over and over. ♡

...
That doesn't explain any-thing.

WH-WHO WOULD EVER BE CRAZY ENOUGH TO DO THAT?!
Y-You don't mean...

"Don't die, Vivian."
"If a woman like you dies, it will be a loss for all of Britannia!"
"No...it will be a loss for me," he uttered.

Dreyfus-sama said *that*?!
He *did* say "This is too cruel," but...
After that, all he did was have Hendrickson cast tons of recovery magic.
LOOM
But it was my dad who treated her in our home afterward.
Listen to this. He literally said that since Vivian had done so much wrong, he couldn't nurse her in the castle, but he also pitied her too much to just let her die.
Whaa-aat?!
Not. To. Mention! The blessed magic of the God-desses...
HA HA HA HA HA!
...even lifted the awful curse that had afflicted my skin. Lucky me! ♡
THAT'S WHAT THEY CALL THE DEVIL'S LUCK.

SNAP
And so...

VRR
I'm over you, Gil!
POKE
I've found true love. ♡

I see now that rather than love another...
GLOOOW
...a woman should *be* loved!

THOUGH I FEEL BAD FOR DREYFUS-SAMA.
I...I don't quite follow, but...
...I guess this is good news for you, Gil?

...
Uh... Gil?

Don't tell me...that all that stalking actually made you start to develop feelings for her...?
No.
THUD
ドスッ

YOU CAN CALL ME
GORILLAMORE.
IT'S GRIA-MORE.
Viv-ian.

What did you mean by what you said earlier?
About "times of chaos."

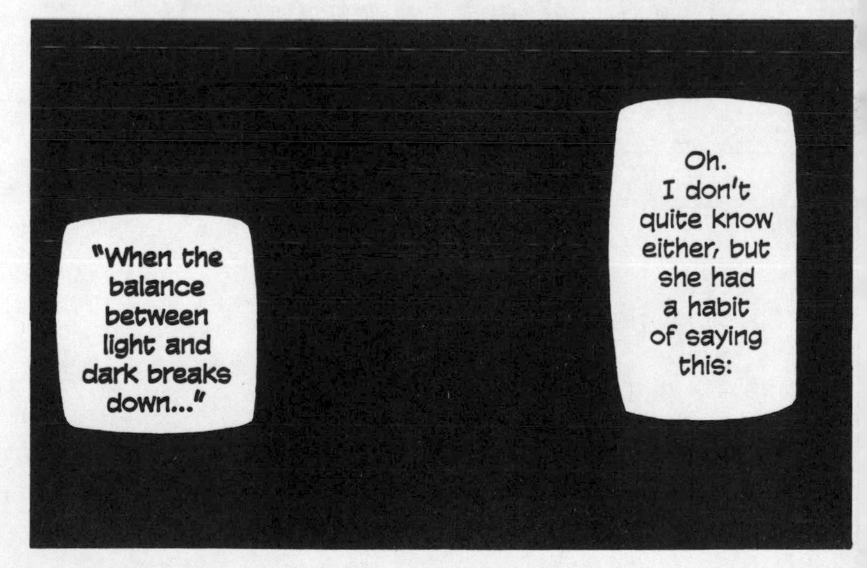
Oh. I don't quite know either, but she had a habit of saying this:
"When the balance between light and dark breaks down..."

"...It will mark the end of the Age of the Gods, and chaos will return."
"Then the world will be reborn."

I don't get it.
Then you can ask her yourself.

Ask the Boar Sin of Greed, Merlin.

THE SEVEN DEADLY SINS

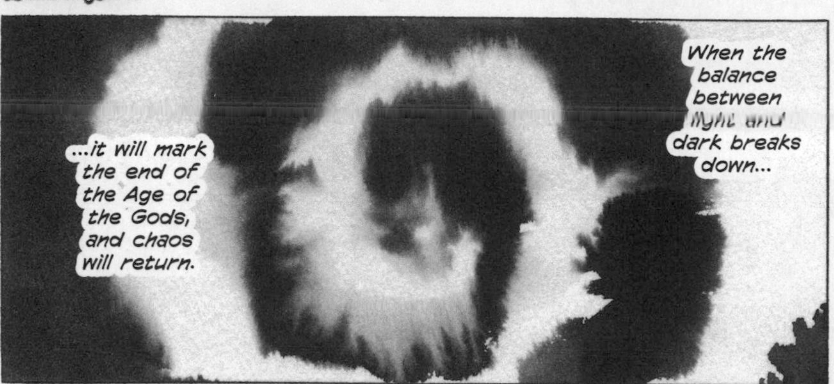
When the balance between light and dark breaks down...
...it will mark the end of the Age of the Gods, and chaos will return.

My gluttonous daughter who is starved for affection and ravenous for knowledge.
You have precipitated that brilliantly.

Chapter 335 - What the Witch Had Always Wanted

Bonus Story: From Another

Drey...fus? Why isn't it...Gil?

Ugh... Water...

Fed directly from... Gil's lips.

I don't care if you're an old man. I'm eating!

So that I can get better and get the heck out of here!

I...I can't help it. It's a natural process.

And the very idea of you watching me while I do it is really... really so very...

I can't help that my body sweats.

And I don't mind. It's nothing you haven't seen already.

Nighty night.

Dreyfus-sama... ♡

The End

GLANCE
CHATTER
CHATTER

PSST
PSST PSST

You see that?
Yeah, what an ugly scar.
I wonder if she can't use her magic to do something about it.

It's a shame, seeing as how she's such a babe.
Agreed.
HMPH.

Hey, Merlin.

This may be none of my business ...
...but I can still heal that burn wound away if you like.
...Is it ugly?

No.
I think it's very beautiful.
If you're okay with it, then so am I.

HOP
Me, too! Me, too! I think it's really striking!
Yeah. I think it's noble to keep it.

AS LONG AS SHE HAS THAT SCAR, ESCANOR STILL LIVES ON IN MERLIN.
HIC!
Tch... You got me there. ♫

Heh heh heh!

Well!
Beauty's in the eye of the beholder.

I miss Escanor, but...

...now everyone can finally be happy.

By using up his Demon Lord powers, the Captain doesn't have to go back to the Demon World.
And Elizabeth's curse has been lifted!

Ban resurrected Elaine, and they get to be together at last.
Could you get me another drink? ♪
Oh, you!
I think that's enough.

Gowther was able to remember his heart and memories of Nadja.
TRUE!

Then...King became the true Fairy King.

And... And I...
...got proposed to by King. ♡
WRIGGLE
WRIGGLE

Proposed to smack dab in the middle of battle. ♫
You're the one that got me going!
GRRR!

And then Merlin...!

Huh?

That reminds me... What is it *you* want, Merlin?
You don't really talk about yourself much, do you?

She'd been helping out the captain and others since way before The Seven Deadly Sins were a thing.
AND THEY KNOW EACH OTHER BEST OF ANYONE ELSE IN THE GROUP.

KAH
KAH!
I can't imagine she'd be the type to help out of sheer goodwill and without any reward for 3,000 years. ♫
Ban!

Hey, Merlin! You have a wish, too, don't you?
Is it some crazy magic experiment? Getting yourself some ultra rare test subjects?!
Tell us! We'll all help you with it!
HEH.

I see.
I suppose you do have a right to know. And an obligation to see it for yourselves...
VRR

SNAP
...as fellow comrades in arms.
WAH!
FWP
!!
MURMUR
Ban... Guys?!

VRR
!!!

Every-one... look!

It's the Boar's Hat!

A...Are we where I think we are?
ZSH
ZSH
Yeah. It's where we were just fighting the Demon Lord earlier.

Look at what's in front of Hawk's mom.

It's the magic lake!

Merlin!
What are you going to start?!
FLAP
FLAP
Now then. Time to get started.
!!

I'm going to awaken Arthur.

!!

AH ...

Arthur ?!

SHWIP
TMP

BOAR HAT

VOOM

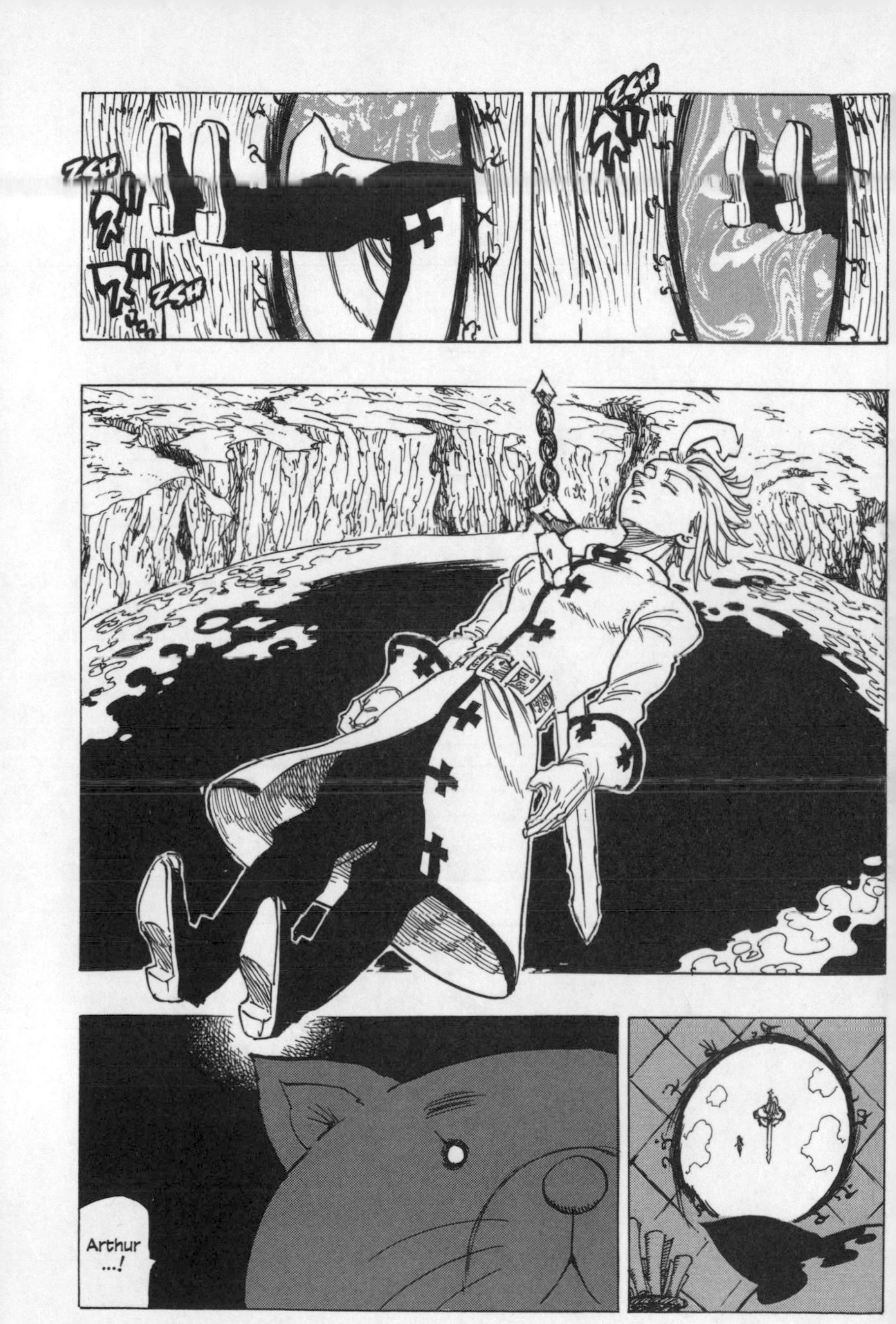
ZSH
ZSH
ZSH
Arthur ...!

She's going to wake up Arthur?
Does she mean... she's going to bring him back to life?
HUH?

I don't know... What's going on?
PEEK
SNOOOOOINK!

You swine!! What took you so long to come for me?!
Hawk?!
Hawk-chan!
CLOP
CLIP
CLOP
CLIP

Nnngggh! I was so lonely, I was trembling all over like a fawn born in the shade of a rock!
Apologize to fawns for that.
MOOSH
BOING
BLOOOP

Huh? You mean you've been here the entire time?
I hadn't even noticed you weren't around...
SORRY.
How cruel!!

When I thought about turning around and going home, my mom suddenly refused to budge from in front of that weird water.
MAS-TER?
I didn't mind coming here with my mom to defeat the Demon Lord, but you guys all beat him up before we even got here!

Hawk, let go of me.
I'll never let go!

I have followed your revela-tion, and now every-thing is in place.
Princess... Are you ready as well?

Hm? "Princess"? Who's Merlin talking to?
WHO KNOWS ...

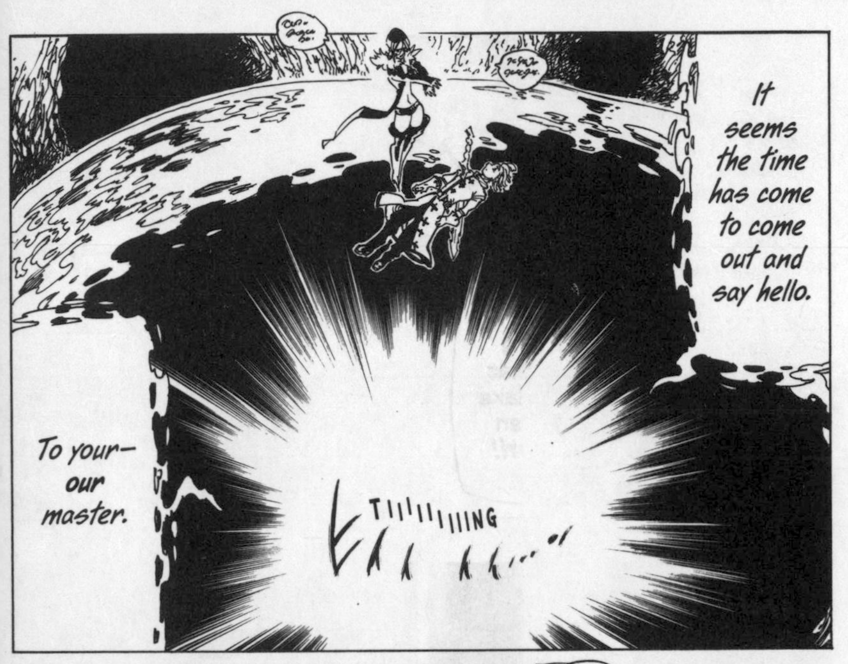
It seems the time has come to come out and say hello.
To your— our master.
TIIIIIIIING

WH-WH-WHO SAID THAT?!
HIC!
Huh? Why's the lake suddenly glowing?
!

Arthur. I was wrong. This wasn't a sword to doom you to death.
It was the key to lead you to the next new stage.

Now, key.
Use the magic that fills the lake and open the door!!

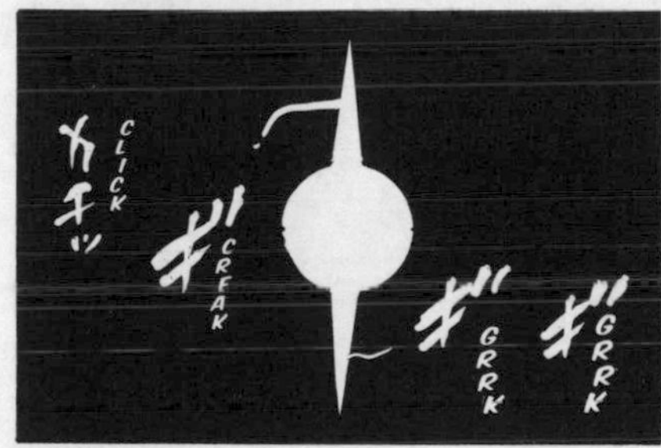
CLICK
CREAK
GRRK
GRRK

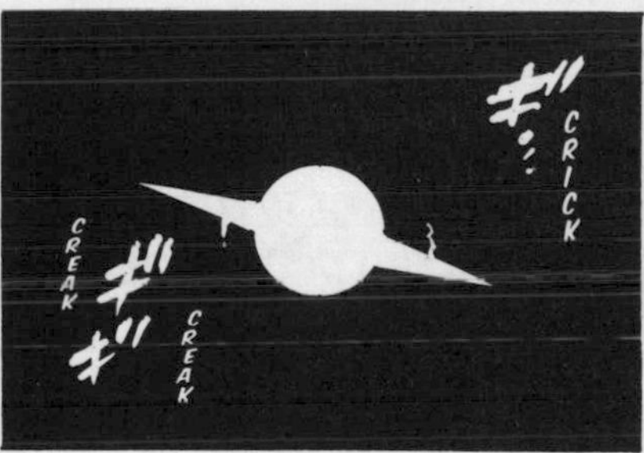
CRICK
CREAK
CREAK

K-CLUNK

BOOM

RRRUMBLE

Wh...
What just hap-pened?

HIC!
Hey. ♫

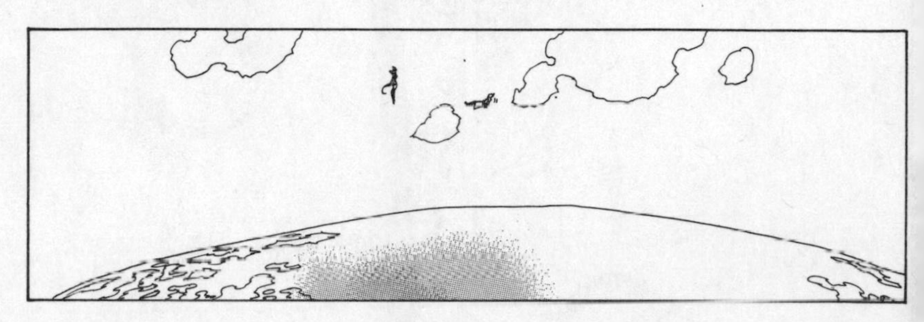

No way! He's alive again!
It's amazing! Arthur's back to life!

Wh...
What...
...was
I doing
...?

Of all the races, Humans are the most contradictory beings, possessing the both extremes of good and evil, light and dark.
And contradiction is no different from chaos. In other words...

...a Human who has been chosen by the Saint of Chaos...
...will become he who com-mands chaos.

Arthur-sama's acting strange ...
Merlin! What are you doing to Arthur?!

I told you. My goal is to awaken Arthur.
AGH ... GUH ...

AS THE LORD OF CHAOS.

Chapter 336 - The Lord of Chaos

Uungh...! Ah...gah! My body...
THROB
What... happened to it?!
THROB
Do not be afraid. Embrace it, Arthur.
It is time for you to awaken to the immeasurable magic concealed within you!
Guuh... uuh!
Merlin... What are you talking...
...
THROB
It hurts...
Help... me...
AUGH!

AUGH!
SNOINK...
OOOO
Meliodas! Arthur-sama's acting strange.
AHH!
M-Mom?! What the heck's the matter?!
OO
AUUU-GGGH!!
When the king awakens, he will release the seal on chaos.
Chaos will return home to the king.
H!
OO

Arthur! Wait!!
BAH

YOU'RE ...!

MELIODAS OF THE DEMON RACE!
I WILL NEVER... LET THE DEMONS HAVE THEIR WAY WITH BRITANNIA!

ズッ
ZSH

Gyaaah! Wh-Wh-What is this?!
Where are we?!
Snoooink! The ground! The ground...!
I-Is everyone okay?!
UH-OH! I DO NOT SEE THE CAPTAIN! OR BAN!
Gowther?! How are you standing there?!
I DO NOT KNOW...
ゴォー GOOOOONG
ゴォー GOOOOONG
What kind of crazy hallucination is this?!
IT IS NOT A HALLUCINATION!
THIS IS... REALITY!

MERLIN! DID YOU DO THIS?!
DSH
WHOOSH
Careful there. ♫
He's really coming after you. ♫

ZOOP
HAA-
AAH!
SSSHH
BASH
Sir Melio-das.

TMP
Ugh!
We met by the guiding hand of a momentous destiny.
So what matters isn't what others think of you, but what you think of others...
THAT VOICE!
ARTHUR, IS THAT YOU?!

Sir Meliodas.
I looked up to you.

So why... Why?!

Listen to me, Arthur.

Meliodas did not betray you.
That is a fact.

Calm down... Don't let you powers consume you.
Come now... It's all right...

Merlin
...

Huh?! What?! What just happened?!
LOOK キョロ
LOOK キョロ
Melio-das, are you okay?!
E-everything's back to normal!
I'm fine.
So... What was all that just now?
I think... that was Arthur's magic!

The Meliodas you met back then is not the true Melio-das.
B-But he betrayed everyone!
You misunderstand. As proof of that, Elizabeth and The Seven Deadly Sins are all here with you.

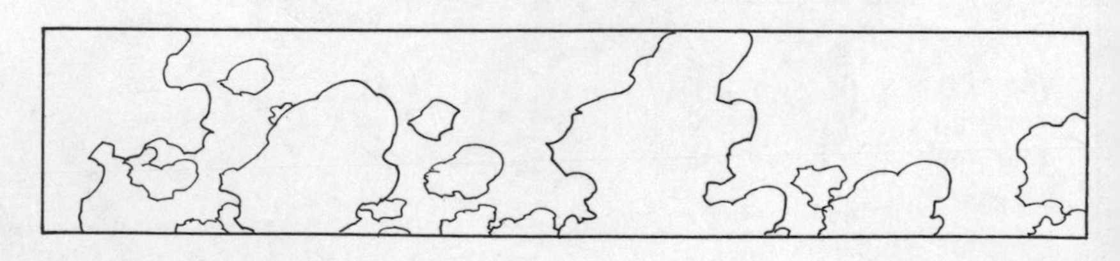

Arthur Pendragon, that was the mistake of a lifetime...
I don't know how I can ever apologize for my error... I'm sorry.
To be honest, my head's still a mess.
You didn't do anything wrong! I'm the one who should be apologizing.
I'm just so happy to see you again!
N-No! Sir Meliodas, you didn't do anything—
Yes! Me, too!
Anyway, there's something I want to ask.

MERLIN. WHAT DID YOU DO TO ARTHUR?
!
WHAT DO YOU MEAN BY "CHAOS"?

Chaos... is an impure and pure entity of darkness that even the Demons fear and light that even the Goddesses worship.
Its power is immense, and it is believed that with a single intention, it brought about this world and all the races from nothingness.

Including the Demon Lord and the Supreme Deity.
!!!

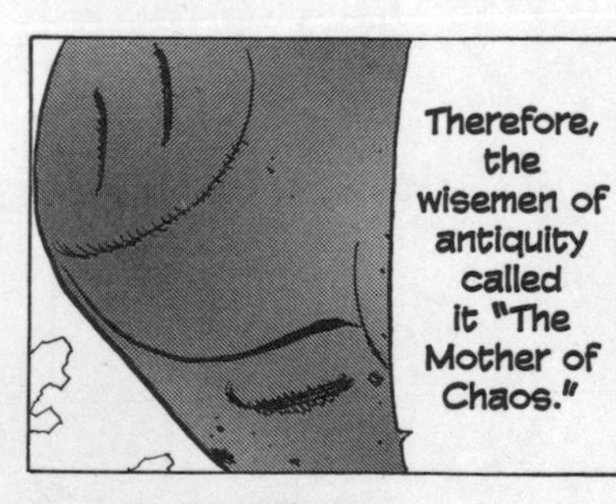
Therefore, the wisemen of antiquity called it "The Mother of Chaos."

Arthur, you command chaos, and are the king who will lead Britannia into a new world.

Merlin... I'm not following what you're saying.
Huh? Me?
Why would you awaken a power that's both a blessing and a curse? What are you plotting?
Is this your wish?!
My wish ...?

Allow me... to answer on Merlin's behalf.

!!!!

I will tell you of the wish made by a single, lonely witch...
...who wandered the land in search of chaos.

Chapter 337 - Merlin

As for why Merlin wanted Chaos...
...I will answer in her place.

Just who are you?! Show yourself!
This smells fishy. ♬

Pardon me this one thing.
For I cannot part from this lake.

I was wrought from Chaos.
The ancients called me "Lady of the Lake" or "The Saint of Chaos."

"Lady of the Lake"...? Where have I heard that before...

Oh, yeah! You're the one who gave the holy sword to King Calphen the First...

Sorry, but I've been around over 3,000 years, and I've never once heard about any being of Chaos.
Let alone from Merlin.

Of course you haven't. That's because for the past 3,000 years, she's hidden it from you and everyone else.
!!

Merlin kept that from us?
WHY IN THE WORLD ...

What are you talking about?

Let me tell you a story of long ago.

Long ago... here in Britannia, there existed a capital blessed with prosperity that sided with neither the Demons nor the Goddesses.
The name of that capital where the superior wisemen of humanity lived was Bérialin.
There, under the pretext of researching the ultimate magic, but really to serve as weapons against the higher ranking Demons and Goddesses...
...Human children who possessed an aptitude for magic were experimented on as test subjects.
Among them, a child was born with the strongest and most unique magic.
Merlin.

From birth, she was a prodigy with a talent and wit that far surpassed the wisemen of the capital.
But inside, she was nothing more than a child hungering for the love of a parent.
However, all that the leader of the wiseman, her father, gave her was a mountain of reading material and tests to perform.
Sick of it all, she up and ran away one day.
Crying, she walked on and on, with no destination in mind.
Her heart was exhausted, and her tears dried up.
Still, she evaded her pursuers and fled, but eventually they caught up to her.
Her days that felt like prison were upon her again...
Or so she thought, when a boy saved her life.

That boy was Meliodas of the Demon race.

The captain saved Merlin?!
OOOOH! ♫ NICE GOING!

I had no idea you'd had such a terrible past.

...It was a long time ago.

When he gently put out his hand, her heart was filled...
...with a love she had never gotten from anyone else.

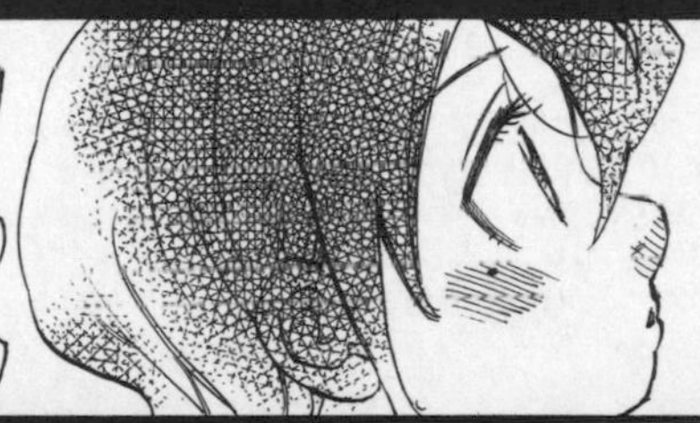
Every time she saw Meliodas, that feeling deepened...
And with time, transformed into something special.

Wait...so Merlin had feelings for the captain?!
N... No way!
Merlin, you...

No matter how much time passed, Meliodas never developed romantic feelings for her.

Merlin worried... and thought... and then decided.

She abandoned her form as a little girl and recreated herself in the image of an adult woman...
...and in order to keep her body like that, she stopped the time that coursed through her.
All so that she could win over Meliodas's heart forever.
But that hope was never realized, and he was stolen by another.

Elizabeth of the God-desses.

Shock... sadness... anger... jealousy.
Young Merlin was assailed by the dizzying maelstrom of feelings.

But she could not bring herself to hate the two of them.
She returned to Bérialin on her own and attempted to fill the gaping hole that had opened in her heart...
...by gobbling up scripts, applying herself to magical training, and greedily devouring all the knowledge of the world.

Chaos.

The drive of power that was born amidst ancient stars far, far away.

It is said that Chaos first created the world.
It birthed the Supreme Deity, the Demon Lord, and its third offspring, the Sacred Tree.

Finally, the Supreme Deity created the Celestial Realm and the Goddess Race.
The Demon Lord created the Demon World and the Demons.
And the Sacred Tree created the Fairy Realm and its Fairy folk.

After that, Chaos created the fourth race: the Giants.

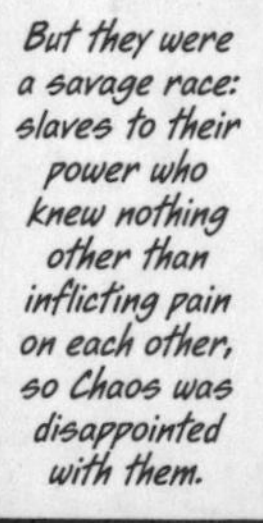
But they were a savage race: slaves to their power who knew nothing other than inflicting pain on each other, so Chaos was disappointed with them.

That's when Chaos created Humans.

They feared that the love and respect their own created races devoted to them...

...would be stolen by their creator, Chaos.

So the Supreme Deity and the Demon Lord worked together to seal Chaos away.

She believed that if she could revive Chaos, who gave rise to virtually endless possibility...
...then her starving heart would most certainly be fulfilled.

...!!

But a number of conditions had to be met for the resurrection to work.
Defeating the Demon Lord was one of them.
Therefore, Merlin used The Seven Deadly Sins.
But she was only evening the ledger, as you all used her plenty as well.

SHUT UP!!

I've stayed quiet and listened to this long enough!
What do you think you know about us?!

S-Sure, there might be a lot of things I don't know...
...but Merlin has fought with The Seven Deadly Sins as a *comrade*! Alongside us!

...Indeed.
It's true that I have not lived with her or even spoken to her.

But as for what I do know...
...I know that it was Merlin who asked the Giant craftsman Dabuzu to forge the Coffin of Eternal Darkness in order to seal away the Demon Lord and the Supreme Deity.

Huh?

Ah, yes. And also...

I know that she intentionally delayed the spell to stop time during the first battle in order to resurrect the Demon Lord.
And that she reactivated the curse on Elizabeth that Meliodas had once broken.
And that in the final battle against the Demon Lord, she drove your combo move into the lake.
That is about all I know.

STOP TALKING NONSENSE! TH...THAT CAN'T BE TRUE...!
Merlin! Stop standing there quietly and say something for yourself!

To revive Chaos, it wasn't enough to seal away the Supreme Deity and the Demon Lord.
One or the other had to be completely destroyed in order to disrupt the balance.

Then you knew the Cap'n's body would be taken over...
...and let him revive that way?

And there was one more condi-tion.
In order to obtain the key to reawaken Arthur, I needed an explosive magic.
But either way, if I hadn't directed the magic into the lake, Britannia would have been destroyed.
THEN ALL THAT THE LADY OF THE LAKE IS SAYING IS...

MER-LIN.
LOOK ME IN THE EYE AND ANSWER ME.

DID YOU REALLY...
...TRY TO KILL ELIZABETH?

Meliodas. Your sole objective was to break the curse on Sissy. But if you'd done that...
...you might have abandoned the mission to defeat the Demon Lord. And I couldn't have that.

You're lying... right?

SO THAT'S WHY YOU REACTIVATED THE CURSE?!
But I'm also the one who saved Sissy!!

CLENCH
Then ...

WHEN YOU ASSEMBLED THE SEVEN DEADLY SINS...
...WAS THAT ALSO ALL TO CARRY OUT YOUR GOAL?!

I thought you were our friend!
HIC!
SOB!

How could you do this to us?!

It should be no mystery.
Hating someone so much you want to kill them but still being able to love them... That's what Humans do.

To Be Continued in Volume 41...

"THE SEVEN DEADLY SINS" ILLUSTRATION CORNER

"THE DRAWING KNIGHTHOOD" SPACE

This is the final Illustration Corner ever! We've run a total of 469 illustrations! Awesome!!

M = H = E = D = B = K = G = Mer = Esc = El = Z =

SPECIAL PRIZE

M "It really has been a wild ride, but we've only made it this far thanks to all you guys! Thank you."

AKITA PREFECTURE / AYANO SUZUKI-SAN

G "Even if my body is artificial and my heart is man-made... I love all of you!"

OSAKA / HARUNA ARA-SAN

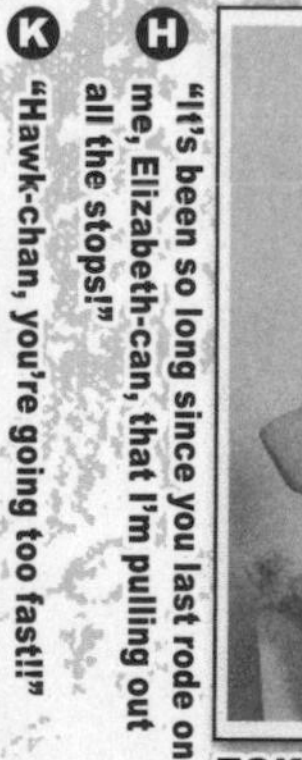

H "It's been so long since you last rode on me, Elizabeth-can, that I'm pulling out all the stops!"

K "Hawk-chan, you're going too fast!!"

TOKYO / LOTTE PIE MOMI-SAN

SAITAMA PREFECTURE / KANNA OYA-SAN

H “Sometimes, I just want to go on a relaxed trip with no drama.”

NAGANO PREFECTURE / WAKIYAKU-SAN

“I hope today can be another day of world peace!”

“You really are one whimsical king.”

Hel “For being a piddly little crybaby, you turned into a fine man, my friend!”

K “Heh heh... Thanks... Hic! (sob)”

SAITAMA PREFECTURE / YUNA KOBAYASHI-SAN

KAGOSHIMA PREFECTURE / HIKARU MIYAHARA-SAN

M “I think your clothes are a little tight on me.”

Z “Don't be a show-off, brother. You and I have almost identical physiques.”

OITA PREFECTURE / HINA FUJITA-SAN

K “Helbram, Oslo, Gloxinia-sama. I will continue to protect the Fairy Realm and the Fairy King's Forest for all of you!”

TOKYO / YUYA KATAYANAGI-SAN

M “I wish I could tell the me from 3,000 years ago how this was the future that lay ahead of me.”

B “Kah kah! ♪ Me, too. ♫”

Mystery "No, no. I'm the one who should be thanking *you*."

El "Ban... Did you hear something just now?"

B "Yeah, I did... Who was that?"

TOKYO / GUDENOKO-SAN

M "Let's go, Zel! We're going to cut the threads of fate trying to control us!"

HYOGA PREFECTURE / MIO OGATA-SAN

SAITAMA PREFECTURE / KK OMOKAGE-SAN

D "When we Seven Deadly Sins act as one, can fight back even the strongest enemy!"

"Meliodas... We're best buds for life, right?"

"You idiot. Of course we are."

SAITAMA PREFECTURE / KAREN SUZUKI-SAN

K "Sorry for making you wait 700 years."

D "Don't worry about it. All that matters is that you came around in the end!"

SAITAMA PREFECTURE / MIKA OZUKA-SAN

M "Me? Wait on Zel? No way, no how!!"

Z "Who're you to decide?!"

Gelda "I don't think it's possible either..."

NIIGATA PREFECTURE / YUKA WATANABE-SAN

FUKUOKA PREFECTURE / HIROTO FUJII-SAN

Demon Lord "Boys! Dinner's ready!"

Z "Just a minute... Let me finish this level!"

M "Same! I'm almost done reading this!"

TOKYO / IYASHINOPE TENSHI-SAN

KING x DIANE

"Hey, King! I think you and I are going to be the strongest married couple the world's ever seen, don't you?!"

MIYAGI PREFECTURE / MIZUKI ABE-SAN

El "Even if I only have a little time left to spend with you, I'm still as happy as I could ever be!"

IWATE PREFECTURE / RYU FLAGGER-SAN

B "I'm convinced that I was put on this earth to meet you. ♪"

El "Oh, Ban...!! (bluuuush)"

MIYAGI PREFECTURE / MAME ENDOU-SAN

D "Yep, yep! King's handsome no matter which version he is!"

H "Huh?"

SAITAMA PREFECTURE / TENGAWA-SAN

El "Look at us all in our bridal gowns!"

Mer "Why are you here?"

G "Ta-daaaa! ☆"

FUKUOKA PREFECTURE / NANAMI KASUGA-SAN

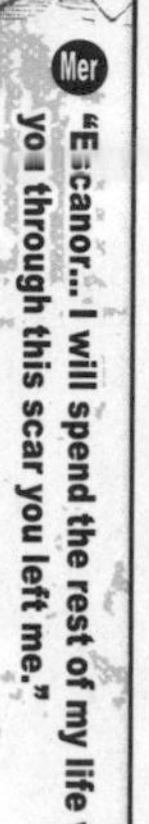

GUNMA PREFECTURE / ANMI-SAN

"Thank you... I'm so glad I fell in love with you, Meliodas!"

HYOGA PREFECTURE / SHIHO OCHIAI-SAN

H "When all this drama's over with, you guys better get hitched!"

Bartra "Waaaaah... Elizabeth!"

NIIGATA PREFECTURE / NANA NAKAGAWA-SAN

I've looked over each and every one of the heartfelt submissions sent in. To those of you who got your works published in the books, those who didn't get to, and those from other countries who joined us, too, you are all the finest of knights! As the leader of the Knighthood of Scraps Disposal, I swear by it! Thank youuuuuuu!!

Deadly Sins"

ENDING

T VOLUME.

JANUARY 2021

Deadly Sins

"The Seven

WILL BE

IN THE NEX

VOL. 41 ON SALE

A Kodansha Comics Trade Paperback Original

Published in the United States by Kodansha Comics, an imprint of Kodansha USA Publishing, LLC, New York.

Publication rights for this English edition arranged through Kodansha Ltd., Tokyo.

First published in Japan in 2020 by Kodansha Ltd., Tokyo as *Nanatsu no taizai*, volume 40.

ISBN 978-1-64651-065-8

Original cover design by Ayumi Kaneko (hive & co., Ltd.)

Printed in the United States of America.

www.kodanshacomics.com

9 8 7 6 5 4 3 2 1
Translation: Christine Dashiell
Lettering: James Dashiell
Editing: Tiff Ferentini
Kodansha Comics edition cover design by Phil Balsman

Publisher: Kiichiro Sugawara

Director of publishing services: Ben Applegate
Associate director of operations: Stephen Pakula
Publishing services managing editor: Noelle Webster
Assistant production manager: Emi Lotto, Angela Zurlo